A PEOPLE IMPRISONED

The Voice of the Martyrs

with Michelle Waters

Living Sacrifice Book Company
Bartlesville, OK 74005

Eritrea: A People Imprisoned

Living Sacrifice Book Company
P.O. Box 2273
Bartlesville, OK 74005-2273

ISBN 978-0-88264-028-0

Edited by Lynn Copeland

Cover design by Lookout Design

Cover creation, page design, and layout by Genesis Group

Printed in the United States of America

Unless otherwise indicated, Scripture references are from the *New King James* version, © 1979, 1980, 1982 by Thomas Nelson Inc., Publishers, Nashville, Tennessee.

About the cover: In the flag of Eritrea, the red triangle stands for the blood lost in the fight for freedom.

"*It's very small numbers [arrested] and we are not shy to say these are individuals who've done harm to the national security of this country. We are not questioning the fact that we have done this and we will continue to do it. This has nothing to do with human rights ... No one has the right to point a finger at us.*"

—PRESIDENT ISAIAS AFEWERKI,
in a rare interview with Reuters, May 2008

"On reflection, I think the authorities should understand by now that what they are doing doesn't work. I am convinced that the number of Christians has doubled or tripled since they closed the churches. So perhaps God is using this terrible situation for his glory."

—HELEN BERHANE,
Eritrean gospel singer

CONTENTS

ACKNOWLEDGMENTS

There are many people who have my deep gratitude for their involvement and support in the writing of this book.

To Riley K. Smith, for your most helpful suggestions and feedback during the writing and editing process. I appreciate your time, your honesty, and your example of steadfast dedication to our suffering brothers and sisters around the world.

To the staff at The Voice of the Martyrs, for providing me the opportunity to share with others these accounts and testimonies of overcoming faith amid terrible suffering. I thank you for your prayers and dedication to this project.

To Lynn Copeland, for your eye for detail and clarifying questions during the editing phase. Your efforts polished the message of this book.

To my family and friends, for your ongoing interest, encouragement, and love. I am truly blessed to have each of you in my life.

Also thanks to the Lord, for guiding my path in introducing me to my persecuted brothers and sisters around the world. My life and faith are richer for knowing their stories and drawing alongside them in their trials and triumphs.

And finally, to each one who reads this book, thank you for taking the time to learn about the difficult reality for Christians in Eritrea today. I pray these pages will, in some small way, inspire you to remember our persecuted brothers and sisters in Eritrea. May you learn from their example and strive to serve God wholeheartedly no matter your circumstances.

MICHELLE WATERS

PROLOGUE:
A STAND FOR FREEDOM

She was just an ordinary woman. But to the state she was a threat.

Helen Berhane once called Eritrea her home. It was in this northeastern African country that she was born, grew up, attended school, and envisioned her future. She was proud of her country and her people. She held her family and her heritage close to her heart.

But closer still she held her relationship with Jesus Christ. Helen grew up in a Christian home and from a young age she embraced the faith as her own. As her country fell into chaos around her, Helen increasingly felt that the Lord was preparing her to suffer for His sake. She accepted this invitation and readied herself. But she had no idea at the time the costly price she would pay for her unwavering devotion.

When Eritrea achieved independence from Ethiopia in the early 1990s, the country was full of optimism. People celebrated; the future looked bright.

Eritrea, a young country, shares much of its history with Ethiopia. It was in Eritrea and northern Ethiopia that the ancient kingdom of Aksum was established. Aksum was later replaced with

Present-day Eritrea

Abyssinia, the name often used for Ethiopia before World War II. During the colonization of Africa, Eritrea was claimed by the Italians. Its future after World War II was decided by the United Nations and it became a federation of Ethiopia. A long war for independence followed, resulting in the deaths of tens of thousands of Eritreans and Ethiopians.

Peace and hope were restored when Eritrea gained independence—or so the people, including Helen, thought. But in 1998 another conflict broke out with Ethiopia. In the two years of fighting, thousands more were killed. Would the country ever experience peace? Was the fighting, the turmoil, finally over?

The Eritrean People's Liberation Front, which was involved in leading the Eritreans to independence, became the ruling party when freedom was established. But quickly, the freedoms Eritreans had fought for and been promised were cruelly taken away by the new regime. Freedom of speech and freedom of religion were dismantled and, piece by piece, Eritrea became one of the most closed and repressed nations in the world today.

For Helen, an ordinary citizen raising a young daughter, the government's crackdown had very real—and very serious—implications. Her personal struggle began in the summer of 2000, when she preached to a group of young people sitting on the steps of a large Catholic church in the country's capital, Asmara. Her heart was overflowing with compassion for these young people, many of whom had known nothing but war in their country. Helen realized that some of these youths might die themselves in the senseless fighting with Ethiopia. She couldn't just walk on by; she had to raise a voice. So she spoke a message of faith, of love, and of peace—urging those listening to pray that the tension between their country and Ethiopia would cease.

When she walked down from the church steps, two members of the secret police grabbed her and brought her to the police station. She was accused of speaking out against the government. Eventually, the officers gave her a warning and released her. But Helen would not let their warnings prevent her from reaching out to fellow Eritreans.

The Eritrean government's crackdown on freedoms became even more severe in the twenty-first century. The press became severely repressed and those who criticized the government found

Helen Berhane and her daughter

themselves arrested, or worse. The government also further suppressed religion in the country. In May 2002, it declared that only four religious groups would be recognized in the country: Islam, the Orthodox Church, the Catholic Church, and the Lutheran-affiliated Evangelical Church. The rest were deemed illegal. Helen, who belonged to a Pentecostal church, suddenly was faced with a choice: give in to the regime and allow them to dictate where and how she could worship, or make a stand for freedom of religion and continue to minister to her fellow citizens.

This was not a decision to be made lightly. The government by this time was arresting people for merely possessing a Bible and was raiding the homes where Christians had gathered to meet together. But Helen continued to serve the Lord as best she could, especially through her gift of song. The policies of the government didn't stop her from writing and composing music. She even continued in her plans to release a gospel album.

Helen's album was released in 2003. Many were blessed by the music, especially a group of young people who asked her to lead a Bible study three times a week in a private home. Helen agreed. But after a month of teaching, Helen's group was discovered by the secret police. She was arrested and brought to the police station. Even there, in a prison cell, Helen sang for various women who had also been imprisoned, blessing them and bringing light to their difficult situations.

Shortly afterward, Helen was transferred to Adi Abeito, a well-known military prison. The suffering on the faces of the other prisoners was plain. Many of them were sick—coughing, vomiting. Helen and some other believers in the prison tried as best they could to care for those who were worse off than they. In particular, there was one man, a Muslim, who was an epileptic. The Christians prayed for him regularly and after he suffered a fit they would wash his bloodied, injured body. He didn't understand why these Christians were helping him. Didn't they have their own problems? Helen shared her faith with him and, using her gift of song, she sang to him. He began to ask more and more about Christianity.

After three weeks at this military camp, Helen was again transferred—this time to Mai Serwa, a camp reserved for dangerous long-term prisoners and serious criminals. She was eventually released from prison and was able to flee the country with her daughter. Helen tells her story in her autobiography, *Song of the Nightingale*.

Helen's story is, unfortunately, not unique. There are hundreds of other Christians who have faced arrest, imprisonment, and torture in Eritrea because of their faith in Christ. At this moment, there are thousands who are facing atrocities in prison for their religious beliefs. This book shares but a few of the stories of our brothers and sisters in Christ throughout the ages who have remained firm in their faith at any cost. May these testimonies inspire you to remember in prayer and in deed the often forgotten Christians in Eritrea. As they suffer, may they know they are not alone.

INTRODUCTION:
A PEOPLE IMPRISONED

Take a moment and picture a metal shipping container—a steel box used for transporting goods
via truck or train. Do you have the image in your
mind? Good. Imagine the shipping container is
rusty in some places. The damp interior has a
dank, metallic smell. The steel, in the warmth of
the sun, is hot to the touch.

Now, imagine being trapped inside the steel
container. You have no water, no food. Picture
yourself in that container on the hottest day of
summer. Now imagine yourself trying to sleep in
the container in the winter, only a thin blanket to
keep you warm.

You have just pictured what is for many believers a daily reality. Today, hundreds are being
held in metal shipping containers that lack proper
ventilation or toilet facilities. Some containers
are overcrowded, with more than a dozen locked
inside. Others are kept in a container all alone for
an undefined amount of time.

In Eritrea, the daytime temperatures can soar
while at night it can become bitterly cold. One
prisoner once said of the containers, "It's like being stuck in an oven in the daytime, and then
overnight it becomes a refrigerator." Prisoners are

Christians have been imprisoned in shipping containers.

held in these containers for hours upon hours at a time, only being let outside temporarily for occasional bathroom breaks and meals. Other prisoners are confined in cells underground, far from the reach of their families and friends. Here they rarely, if ever, see the sunshine.

Can you imagine?

The conditions inside these "prisons" are absolutely atrocious. Often their only toilet is a bucket in the corner of the cell. A few times a day, they are brought to an open field to relieve themselves—but always they are under the watchful eyes of armed guards. Diarrhea is a continual problem for many; prisoners who experience such ailments have no choice but to overcome the shame and embarrassment of no privacy, no discretion whatsoever, during their bouts of sickness.

Food is in short supply, and the meager portions prisoners receive hardly make for a balanced diet. Prisoners eat mostly dry bread, occasionally receiving other items like lentils.

In such an environment, it is common for prisoners to experience various sicknesses, including malaria. Authorities, intent on making believers recant, have been known to deny medical treatment to those suffering illnesses unless they agree to deny Christ.

Senait Oqbazgi Habta died in the Sawa Military Training Center in April 2010 after suffering abuse and being denied medical treatment for malaria and severe anemia. Senait was arrested in 2008, along with fifteen other university students, for attending a Bible study group. Officials at the camp reportedly offered her freedom and medical attention if she would only renounce her faith in Christ. She refused. Eventually the camp officials did relent and allowed her to be moved to the prison's medical center, but it was too late. Senait died a short time later. She was only twenty-eight.

Only a month earlier, another prisoner, Efrem Habtemichel Hagos, died while in solitary confinement in the Adi-Nefase military camp in Assab. His death was caused by malaria and pneumonia, which he had been suffering with for three months. He was reportedly denied proper medical treatment because he too refused to give up his faith in Jesus.

Torture is another method officials routinely use to punish, intimidate, or coerce prisoners. One of the most common forms of torture, called "the helicopter," involves tying up a prisoner's hands and feet behind his back with rope. The victim is left outside in this contorted position for days or even weeks at a time, being untied for only a few moments throughout the day. Other forms of torture include beatings, electric shocks, and sexual abuse.

In January 2010, a Christian woman died of a heart attack at the Alla military camp after suffering torture from prison officials. Hana Hagos Asgedom, age forty-one, was placed in solitary confinement when she refused to recant. In the days before her death, she was beaten with an iron rod for not agreeing to "make the chief commander in the camp a cup of coffee"—an order local Christians believe was really a sexual advance. She was returned to her cell where she endured further punishment and later died.

For many of us, we can only imagine what it would be like to face these conditions. But for hundreds of Christians in Eritrea, the abuse and abysmal surroundings are their reality. For hundreds of other believers, they live with the knowledge that their mother, father, sibling, pastor, or friend may be enduring conditions like these—simply because they believe in Jesus Christ and refuse to compromise their faith and convictions.

Can you imagine?

ARRIVAL OF CHRISTIANITY AND MISSIONARIES (4TH–9TH CENTURIES)

Although Eritrea is a young country, its location along the Red Sea has been the home of various peoples and kingdoms throughout the ages. Christianity was introduced to the area in the fourth century and the faith spread significantly in the years to come. In time, the Orthodox church in the area we know today as Eritrea was visited by missionaries who shared their own interpretations and traditions with the people. The reaction to the missionaries was often mixed. There were those who appreciated the ideas and theology the missionaries brought, but others were content with their Orthodox tradition and felt the missionaries were stirring up dissention.

This struggle continues to this day in Eritrea, where the government looks with suspicion on "new" or "imported" faiths and permits only religious groups that are considered traditional to Eritrea. To explore the struggles the church and believers have faced in Eritrea, let's begin with the introduction of Christianity to the area in the fourth century.

Christianity Arrives in Aksum

The two Syrian boys were on a boat heading back home when calamity struck. It was the fourth century, and the two, Frumentius and Aedisius, suddenly found themselves in an unfamiliar kingdom to the west of the sea—Aksum, an ancient state located in present-day Eritrea and northern Ethiopia. The boys were brought before the kingdom's ruler, Emperor Ella Amida, who made them his slaves. But despite their captivity, Frumentius and Aedisius freely shared their faith with others.

When Frumentius was eventually freed from being a slave, he went to the church leader in Egypt to request a bishop be sent to Aksum. He didn't want to leave Aksum without a Christian leader to guide the growing community of believers.

The church leader in Egypt did meet with Frumentius and listened as he recounted his life and work in Aksum. The church leader then made his decision: a bishop would indeed be sent to Aksum, and that bishop would be Frumentius himself! The church leader then consecrated Frumentius and sent him back. The boy who arrived in Aksum as a slave returned as its bishop.

In the years that followed, Christianity spread rapidly. Eventually, the emperor's son converted to the faith and the kingdom followed suit, becoming known as a Christian state.

Through Bishop Frumentius, the church in Aksum became intrinsically linked for centuries to the Orthodox, or Coptic, church in Egypt. When a new bishop, known as an *abuna*, was required in Aksum, a request would be made to the church leader in Egypt to commission and dispatch the new leader. At times, the relationship between Aksum and Egypt would prove difficult, as communicating with the church leader in the faraway land of Egypt was not always possible.

The Arrival of Catholic Missionaries

Catholic missionaries began to arrive in the kingdom in the sixteenth century. By then, Aksum had slowly waned and had been replaced by Abyssinia. A Jesuit bishop, Andre de Oviedo, arrived in the country in 1557 to begin his missionary work. However, the relationship between Abyssinia's Christians, who were Orthodox, and the Jesuit missionaries quickly soured due to some of the missionaries' confrontational tactics.

In the seventeenth century, the Jesuit missionaries were ordered to leave the country by the emperor. Those who stayed risked death if they were found. In 1640, the remaining Catholic missionaries in Abyssinia were put to death. One of the missionaries who fled the country during this time was Antonio d'Andrade. Later, he was made a bishop and returned to minister in Abyssinia. In 1670, he was martyred in the port city of Massawa in present-day Eritrea.

Abyssinians who had converted to Catholicism were not safe either. If they didn't agree to renounce their new faith, they were either exiled or murdered by the country's authorities. Some stayed in the country, working underground under the leadership of Father Nogueira, who was later discovered and killed.

For approximately two hundred years, Abyssinia attempted to close itself off from other foreign influences. However, the small Catholic community that had survived the exiles and massacres was able to hold on to its presence in the country.

The First Protestant Missionary

After the Catholics were expelled from the country, another visitor arrived in Abyssinia: a German man named Peter Heyling. Peter—a doctor, lawyer, and lay theologian—arrived in Abyssinia sometime in the 1630s.

Peter is likely best known for his work in translating the Scriptures. Passionate in his view that the church should teach people directly from the scriptures, he began translating the gospel into the language many people could understand: Amharic. At the time, church liturgy was most always spoken and written in Ge'ez.

But only a year later, Peter's welcome in Abyssinia was overstayed. Several church leaders were upset with Peter and his emphasis on the Scripture. More and more, the emperor was pressured to take action against Peter. Sometime in the early 1650s, Peter left Abyssinia for Egypt. On his way, Peter was stopped by the Turkish *pasha* (a high-ranking member of the Ottoman Empire) of Suakin, which was a port city along the Red Sea north of Eritrea in present-day Sudan. The *pasha* gave him a choice: convert to Islam or die. Peter chose to become a martyr for his faith. It would be a number of years before Protestant or Catholic missionaries ministered again in Abyssinia.

Protestant Missionaries Return

For approximately forty years at the beginning of the nineteenth century, the church did not receive an *abuna* from Egypt. In addition, learning diminished within the country and fewer people studied Ge'ez, the language most often used for religious purposes. Many Abyssinians, either confused or uninterested in the church and its ongoing theological disputes, turned instead to Islam. It was at this low time in Abyssinia's history that Protestant and Catholic missionaries were finally able to again enter and work within the country.

In the 1800s, several missionaries arrived from Europe, with more to follow in the coming years. They focused on spreading copies of the Scriptures in Amharic so that people could understand God's Word for themselves.

Catholic Missionaries Return

Catholic missionaries during this time were also very much active in working among the Abyssinian people. In 1839, a Catholic missionary by the name of Justin de Jacobis arrived in the north. De Jacobis sought to reach the people by assimilating into their culture to better relate to them. Before long, monks in the country and common people began to follow de Jacobis. Even Ghebra-Mika'el, a very well educated and esteemed monk from Gondar, converted to Catholicism.

Another Catholic missionary, Bishop Massaja, also worked closely with de Jacobis in the north. However, the Turks, who had occupied the coast, soon exiled him from Massawa. He returned several times, but was eventually banished from the country.

Suspicion of Foreign Influences

Throughout history, many rulers of the areas of present-day Eritrea have looked with suspicion on foreign influences, including the beliefs and practices of Catholic and Protestant missionaries. This suspicion of "foreign" faiths echoes today in present-day Eritrea, where the state has repressed unregistered religious groups in the country that do not conform to the four recognized faith traditions.

THEY WAIT, THEY HOPE,
THEY PRAY

All they could find of him was his abandoned car.

One ordinary Friday in March 2005, Kidane Weldou, a senior pastor of the unregistered Full Gospel Church, just...disappeared. In the heart of Asmara, the country's capital, he went missing—presumably snatched by authorities.

For the rest of the weekend, officials gave no word to his family or church about what happened. His loved ones searched for him in vain, finding only his vehicle—empty, with no clues as to where, or why, he was taken.

Kidane's family and friends had good reason to suspect the government's involvement in his disappearance. In the months before he was taken, other senior leaders of the Full Gospel Church were also apprehended. Several of these Christian leaders remain in prison to this day. It is assumed that Kidane suffered a similar fate—that somewhere in the

Image courtesy of Compass Direct News

Pastor Kidane Weldou

east African country of Eritrea he is being held in detention.

Pastor Weldou is married and has four daughters. For more than five years now they have waited, hoped, and prayed that, one day, their husband and father will be returned to them.

THE SPREAD OF ISLAM
(7TH–19TH CENTURIES)

The prosperity Aksum enjoyed with its relative stability and profitable trade routes along the Red Sea began to crumble in the seventh century. Across the Red Sea in Arabia, the religion of Islam was growing. In time, Muslims gained more and more control of the port cities along the coast in present-day Eritrea, giving them increasing control of the trade routes.

By the eighth century, Arabs professing the Islamic faith had also arrived at the Red Sea coast and settled on the Dahlak islands near the port city of Massawa. Conversions to Islam were slow, but over time several of the people groups along the coast converted to Islam. Aksum, either unwilling or lacking the muscle to push back the growing Muslim presence, retreated inland toward the south.

Islam was also expanding throughout the rest of the world, and Christians increasingly felt the pressures of this new religion. In the Middle East, for example, Muslims had conquered what were once mainly Christian countries. Only a handful of Christian states remained. In Africa, the only other Christian country was Nubia, an ancient kingdom located in present-day Sudan.

But then Nubia fell, conquered by the Baybars in the 1270s. Only Abyssinia remained as a Christian nation, a bastion among growing Muslim states.

Aksum's withdrawal during this period also meant that the church lost touch for years, sometimes decades, at a time with Egypt, the place where their *abunas* were selected and commissioned. When Arab Muslims took over Egypt, it only increased the difficulty of communicating with the church there. At times, communication was all but cut off.

The Jihad of Ahmad Gragn

In the sixteenth century, Abyssinia faced its greatest challenge yet—*jihad* from Adal, the Muslim state to the east, which was located in modern-day Somalia. The growing tensions between Muslims and Christians culminated into a religious fervor under the military leader Ahmad ibn Ibrihim al-Ghazi, called Gragn, the "left-handed."

Gragn was a military man, a fearless combatant that soldiered for Adal and rallied the people under the banner of Islam. When Gragn stopped paying a tax to Abyssinia's emperor, Lebna Dengal, the emperor responded with force. But Gragn and his men were ready. They not only withstood the emperor's army, they fought back and won. With a victory under his belt, and to hold the devotion of his men, Gragn declared *jihad*, or holy war, on Abyssinia. In 1528, the emperor fought Gragn in the decisive battle of Shimbra Kure.

Despite Dengal's larger army, the Muslim forces were tightly united and had a strong military mind at the helm. The Muslims claimed the victory, although the emperor did survive, allowing Gragn and his men to overtake wide areas of the kingdom over the next few years. Gragn's control spread across the central regions of Abyssinia and into areas around the Red Sea, including regions of modern-day Eritrea and northern Somalia.

In the northern areas of present-day Eritrea, *jihad* was slower to arrive. As the Muslims steadily made their way up north after winning victories in other parts of Abyssinia, they wrought

Ahmad Gragn

destruction on the country—razing churches, monasteries, and other religious sites in their path. Religious manuscripts, art, and relics from Abyssinia's long history were destroyed or lost, never to be recovered in the same capacity. Some monks, devastated by the destruction, chose to burn along with the items pillaged from their churches and monasteries. It was a substantial loss not only for the Christian people, but also for the country—in a matter of years, the kingdom lost centuries of learning, culture, and experience.

When the Muslims eventually reached the north, Gragn set up a puppet ruler from the family of a Christian nobleman to serve as governor and keep an eye on his newly won territory. The people felt defeated. Some regions of the north agreed to pay Gragn the tax he imposed on them, but others refused. Gragn's Muslim forces inhabited the northern regions for approximately a year. However, they had to leave the area due to a severe shortage in supplies and an outbreak of sickness. In fact, the situation was so difficult and strenuous that many Muslims in Gragn's ranks converted to Christianity.

By 1540, Gragn considered himself ruler of Abyssinia—and many of the people accepted his command. Instead of standing in opposition, many stood by and allowed the rampant destruction to occur around them. Tens of thousands converted to Islam in order to save their lives, while countless others were sold into slavery—a profitable market at the time.

In 1541, four hundred Portuguese troops arrived at Massawa after the emperor sent a plea asking for their help. Pushing inward toward the highlands, the Portuguese and the beleaguered Abyssinian people gathered and defeated Gragn in battle. However, Gragn was not without his own allies. In the sixteenth century, Portugal and Turkey were both seeking control and profit from the Red Sea trade routes. Recognizing the benefit in supporting Gragn's campaign, the Turkish Ottomans answered his request for assistance in the form of eight hundred men and ten cannons. With Ottoman support in tow, Gragn had an army Abyssinia could not restrain, even with help from the Portuguese. In 1542, Gragn won a noteworthy battle. Among the wounded was the leader of the Portuguese troops, Cristovao da Gama.

Confident that he had conquered his foes, Gragn dismissed the Ottoman troops and sent them home. But the Abyssinians and Portuguese assembled their remaining men to attack Gragn. In February 1543, Gragn and his army, caught off-guard and lacking the Ottoman resources, were overcome. Gragn was killed in the battle and, without a visible leader, his men fled. The years of holy war—of *jihad*—were over.

Peace was restored to Abyssinia, but irreparable damage to the country had been done. Over time, the kingdom did indeed grow stronger but never to the same extent as in earlier centuries. *Jihad* had left a deep scar on Abyssinia and the foundation of its church was shaken. Yet the church was not destroyed, and many of those who had converted to Islam recognized their error and turned back to Christ.

The emperor, however, was not quick to receive all the newly reconverted Christians. Some who pled for his mercy were allowed to live but others were beheaded for their betrayal. The people were expected to be loyal to their emperor, and it seems that this included their loyalty to the Christian faith. A Portuguese author at the time noted that if the emperor had killed all those who asked for forgiveness, there would be no one but the emperor left in the kingdom. During the long and difficult years of *jihad*, the light of Abyssinia, the sole Christian kingdom among the African nations, had wavered—had nearly been extinguished—but did not go out.

The Ottoman Empire Claims the Coast

Even though the *jihad* was over, Muslim influence in Abyssinia was there to stay. In 1557—the same year bishop Andre de Oviedo arrived in Abyssinia—the Ottomans gained control of Massawa, an important port in present-day Eritrea, as well as a large area of coastal plains in the north. Despite the attempts of multiple emperors to oust the Muslims, several regions in the north remained under Ottoman control until the nineteenth century.

THE PERSECUTION
OF QUEEN GUDIT

When the ancient kingdom of Aksum began to diminish in size and power in the seventh century, the safety for Christians there also began to waver. Over the next centuries, Aksum slowly shifted away from the north and moved south toward the lands of the Agew people.

The Agew people resisted the newcomers to their lands. In particular, legends tell of an Agew queen, named Gudit, who unleashed havoc on the Christians in the area sometime during the tenth century. Queen Gudit is likely based on several different Agew rulers, since the events attributed to her cover too long a span to have been performed by one monarch.

But whether a single queen or a series of monarchs, the destruction on the church during her rule was severe. Church buildings were destroyed, including a cathedral in the northern city of Aksum, and thousands of believers were allegedly killed.

At this time, Aksum was already vulnerable. These attacks further weakened what was once a powerful nation and an established church.

MY STRENGTH, MY SONG: A REFUGEE'S STORY

"Miriam" (not her real name) ushered the two VOM staff members into her living room and invited them to sit down. Photos of her children, one girl and three boys, adorned the walls. Miriam's youngest, an outgoing toddler, observed the visiting women warily at first, but then moved closer to examine their notebooks and clipboards. In the background a children's DVD was playing on the television. "He just loves to watch these videos," Miriam told her guests. The video was made in Eritrea, the country Miriam and her children once called home.

Miriam fled Eritrea with her children in early 2008. Their first year in Canada was challenging—learning a different language and adjusting to a new culture and surroundings. But most difficult was building a life without "Peter" (not his real name), Miriam's husband and the children's father, who they hope will one day be able to join them in Canada.

Peter learned about Jesus at the Christian orphanage where he grew up and became a believer as a child. Later, in his twenties, he met Miriam through a mutual friend. Miriam began to attend church with him and came to faith in Christ. A year later, the two married in the church where Peter was pastor.

In 2002, when Eritrea began to crack down on evangelical Christians throughout the country, Miriam shredded Peter's graduation certificate from Bible college so there would be no proof that he had ever attended. By that time, Peter was traveling throughout Eritrea sharing the Good News and was well-known as a pastor. In 2006, he was imprisoned for five months. Upon his release he fled to Sudan. And disappeared.

Shortly after Peter fled the country, Miriam was arrested and was placed in detention for twenty days. Deprived of food and water, she was blindfolded and tied to a pole for extended periods in the hot sun. She endured whipping and verbal assaults. As Miriam spoke of her horrific experience, the staff members could see the pain on her face. She expressed to them the guilt she felt for not speaking out about Jesus while she was in prison. "Those who talked openly about Jesus were given the worst treatment. I had Jesus in my heart but I kept thinking about my children at home. If something happened to me, who would care for them?"

When Miriam was released, she and her children fled the country. It took them five long days to drive to Sudan. When they arrived, they were confined in a friend's home for approximately seven weeks while fake passports were created for them. A man was hired to bring Miriam and the children to Canada and to help them through customs. However, when they arrived at Pearson International Airport in Toronto, the man abandoned the family—leaving them without money or any idea where to go or who to turn to. "We had nothing," Miriam told the women. "I could not speak the language. I just cried and cried, not knowing what would happen to me and my children. I cried out to God, asking Him to help us."

Eventually Miriam met a man from Sudan at the airport and pleaded with him to help. When it was suggested that they go to the police, Miriam's children were terrified. In Eritrea, police are the ones who take parents away from children and split families apart. But they had little choice and were amazed at the kindness shown to them.

After Miriam had been in Canada for some time, she heard from a trusted source that her husband had been kidnapped while in Sudan and brought back to Eritrea, presumably to jail. Although she hasn't heard confirmation, she has hope that he is still alive.

When the staff members asked Miriam how those around the world could pray for her family she told them, "Please pray for my husband. Pray especially for his protection, for his good health. Pray that he will feel God's presence in his life."

Miriam is now building a new life for her children in Canada. With help from The Voice of the Martyrs she applied and was approved for permanent resident status. An application was also made for Peter, as Miriam and her children remain hopeful that he is alive and that they will one day be reunited in Canada.

This family now lives in a comfortable home near the children's schools and the church that has warmly embraced them. Miriam volunteers at her church and has built many strong friend-ships—especially with other women who have also had to flee their home countries.

As Miriam and the women from VOM sat together, Miriam's youngest son crawled into her lap and she spoke to him softly in their native

Miriam and her son

language. Times have been hard for this family and they will undoubtedly face more difficult days. Miriam longs to see her husband again; the children miss their father deeply. But it was clear that they felt the Lord's hand in their lives. Miriam told the women that she will continue to give Him the praise and the glory for His provision and love. "I know it's all from God, all from Him," she told them, smiling a wide and beautiful smile.

* * *

"The LORD is my strength and song,
and He has become my salvation;
He is my God, and I will praise Him;
my father's God, and I will exalt Him."

—EXODUS 15:2

THE FIGHT
FOR FREEDOM

By the mid-nineteenth century, Abyssinia was surrounded on all fronts by foreign forces. The northern coast, as it had been for hundreds of years, was dominated by the Ottoman Empire, although its power was now in a period of decline.

In 1865, Turkey handed Massawa over to the Egyptians. But then, in the 1930s, the Italians invaded the land and seized control. Eritrea, Abyssinia, and Somaliland were considered provinces of Italian East Africa.

The time of Italian colonization also affected the church in Eritrea, making it very difficult to maintain any relationship with Egypt, which the Orthodox church relied on for its leadership. Instead, Eritrea's church leadership was handed over in the 1890s to the Italian Capuchins. The Lazarists, the small Catholic community in the country that survived after de Jacobis was expelled, were also soon forced to leave the area.

The Future Decided
The tides turned when World War II erupted and the Allied troops ousted the Italians from their colonies. Eritrea was handed over to the British to govern until a decision could be made about its future by the United Nations.

For ten years, the future of Eritrea was in limbo. Foreign superpowers like Britain and the United States voiced their opinions about Eritrea's future, mostly in line with what would best suit their own needs. Meanwhile, the voices of the Eritreans themselves were largely ignored, despite their best efforts to make their wishes known. Many pushed for independence, wishing

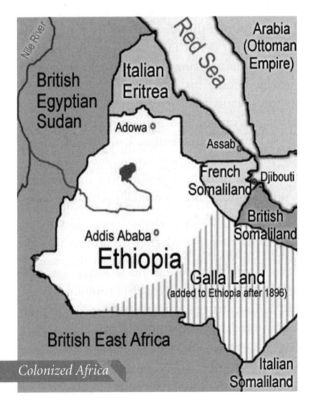

Colonized Africa

to be recognized as a separate country, a unique people. During this time there was conflict between many Muslims, who wished for independence, and many Christians, who saw the appeal in joining with the Christian nation of Ethiopia. Regardless of their stance, the pleas of Eritreans fell on deaf ears.

In 1950, the United Nations announced their decision: Eritrea would become an autonomous federation of Ethiopia. But before long, Haile Selassie, the ruler of Ethiopia, began dismantling the federation, seeking to make Eritrea just another province under his rule. In 1962, a vote about Eritrea's status was taken in both Addis Ababa, Ethiopia's capital, and Asmara, Eritrea's capital. With Ethiopian authorities strongly pressuring the voters, the result was unanimous: the federation was turned down and Eritrea was annexed with Ethiopia. Eritrea was no longer a federation, it was a province.

A Thirty-Year Battle

Even before the vote that made Eritrea another province of Ethiopia, there were rumblings of an impending struggle for independence. Ethiopia had made clear its intentions to win Eritrea as its own—how were the Eritrean people going to respond? In the early 1960s, a nationalist and Marxist guerrilla war began against Ethiopia. One of these pro-independence groups was called the Eritrean Liberation Front (ELF). At first, the predominately Muslim group did not allow Christians to join. Some who tried to were executed. Another such group was the Eritrean People's Liberation Front (EPLF).

In the fight for independence, which lasted a long thirty years, both armed groups and the government committed grave human rights violations. Christians, too, were targeted and suffered in the years of chaos. In 1971, over fifty Christians were burned to death in Debre Sila when they didn't give the ELF a tax payment that was demanded. The ELF also ordered that Christian missions in the area hand over cash and medicines.

Finally, in 1991, Eritrea gained its freedom. In the process, the EPLF discarded the Marxist beliefs they once espoused. Independence was officially recognized two years later, in 1993, after a referendum supervised by the United Nations took place. The vote was overwhelmingly in favor of an independent Eritrea.

At last they were free! But their freedom was short-lived. Already in 1998 the two countries were again at war with one another. After two years, war ended when Eritrea and Ethiopia signed a peace treaty, yet to this day the relationship between countries remains tenuous.

"WE ASK NOT FOR THEIR RELEASE, BUT THAT THEY WOULD REMAIN BOLD FOR JESUS"

The pastors were at their homes with their families when police arrived in the early hours on a Sunday in May 2004. Authorities seized the men, Haile Naizgi and Dr. Kiflu Gebremeske, and brought them to separate police stations. The wives and children of the pastors must have been terrified. *Where are you taking him? What wrong has he done?* Before dragging the pastors away, the officials threatened the women and confiscated the keys to the pastors' offices at the church.

How could these men—ordinary husbands and fathers—be considered a threat? How could a country so ravaged by war and conflict now turn against these peaceful Christian leaders and find fault worthy of arrest on an early Sunday morning?

The problem, in the eyes of the state, was that both men were pastors of the Full Gospel Church, one of Eritrea's largest Pentecostal denominations—a denomination not recognized as one of the four approved religious institutions. Worshiping outside the state-recognized groups was bad enough—*leading* within a rogue religious denomination was blatant dissent.

At a meeting called by the government's Department of Religious Affairs a month before the pastors' arrest, they, along with other local Protestant leaders, were warned: "Do not inform anyone outside Eritrea of your problems." They were also forbidden to invite Christian speakers from abroad without first getting government permission. It was just another step in the government's clampdown on freedom within the country.

The pastors must have known the danger, felt the tightening restrictions on speech and religion, but those at the meeting refused to give in to the government's demands. They declared they would continue to tell the outside world about what was going on in Eritrea until their legal and constitutional rights to freedom of worship were restored.

The government responded to their defiance by committing further violations of rights: they gave no reason for arresting Haile and Dr. Kiflu and continued to hold them without charge or trial. Eventually, the families of the pastors were permitted to bring them food and clothing, but were not allowed to see

Image courtesy of Compass Direct News

Dr. Kiflu Gebremeske

them face-to-face. The pastors' loved ones un-doubtedly prayed intently and without ceasing. One of the pastors' friends shared his prayer request, a plea that echoed the deep faith of the arrested men: "We ask not for their release, but that they would remain bold for Jesus."

Only months later, in August, the families of the pastors discovered that the men had been transferred from their police cells in Asmara to an unknown location. Today, the whereabouts of these pastors continues to be unknown. Where are they being held, and are they even alive?

Haile Naizgi

Image courtesy of Compass Direct News

Continue to pray, trusting that the Lord knows their whereabouts and condition. Pray for these pastors and the others like them who are being held illegally without charge in Eritrea's deplorable prisons. Pray for their release, but even more so, join our Eritrean brothers and sisters in praying that the pastors remain bold in their faith in Jesus, despite the long years of isolation and persecution they have endured.

DELIVERERS
TO DESPOTS

After years of fighting with Ethiopia, Eritrea was at last liberated and free—or so its people thought. But independent Eritrea did not become the place of freedom its citizens had fought and died for. The Eritrean people instead witnessed their country's so-called deliverers, the EPLF, emerge as a repressive regime.

Upon independence, the EPLF became the ruling party in the country, taking on the name the Popular Front for Democracy and Justice (PFDJ). *Democracy? Justice?* The party has since failed abysmally in promoting or protecting these ideals for the people. Instead, the PFDJ clamped down on freedom and human rights, effectively making the country a prison for many Eritreans. The PFDJ's leader, Isaias Afewerki, who remains the current president of the country, stated in a public speech on March 5, 2004, that some religious groups in the country were being beguiled by foreigners to "distract from the unity of the Eritrean people and distort the true meaning of religion." He went on to report that such "futile efforts" would not be permitted.

One of the first initiatives of the PFDJ was to quash any dissenting voices in the country and in the press. In 1994 the party had shut down the main Catholic and Evangelical Lutheran publications. After achieving independence, they continued the media closures, especially as journalists began to openly criticize their new government. By 2001, all independent media was terminated, making Eritrea the only country in Africa without privately owned media.

The government also severely restricted nonprofit groups in the country, including church-run humanitarian projects. The Kale Hiwot Church, a large Protestant denomination, saw their humanitarian and development projects shut down and their assets confiscated by the government. All other independent organizations in the country were forcibly closed, while international groups were forbidden from entering or working within Eritrea.

A New Threat

Within a few years, the Eritrean government saw another threat among their people: religious minorities, including the dozen or so other evangelical and independent denominations. Such groups, which comprise approximately 2 percent of the population, include Anglican, Presbyterian, Adventist, Assemblies of God, Methodist-linked, and indigenous Pentecostal and charismatic congregations.

In an unexpected statement in May 2002, the government announced that only four religious groups would be recognized. The other religious institutions would be required to apply for registration from the newly created Department of Religious Affairs. The four recognized groups were the Eritrean Orthodox church (which had split

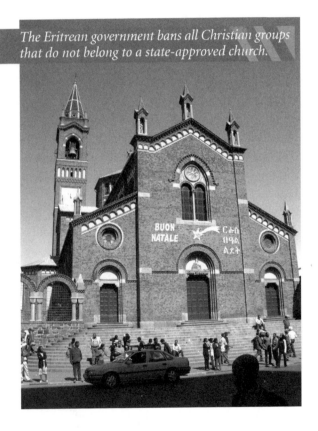

The Eritrean government bans all Christian groups that do not belong to a state-approved church.

from the Ethiopian Orthodox church upon independence), the Eritrean Catholic church, Sunni Islam, and the Lutheran-affiliated Evangelical church. The other Christian churches were suddenly deemed illegal. That year, many church buildings were shut down by authorities.

Several of the unrecognized Christian groups attempted to apply for registration from the government. However, they ran into a problem: the Department of Religious Affairs made no acknowledgment of receiving applications and provided no communication or follow-up with the applicants. Today, there are still only four registered groups; none of the other religious communities in Eritrea have been "approved" by the government.

Some other religious communities were hesitant to even apply for registration, as the government required applicants to provide the names of church members and information about foreign aid they had received. After all, the PFDJ had not shown themselves to be the beacon of freedom and liberty the people expected. Could the government be trusted with the names of people belonging to "illegal" religious groups? Some denominations thought it better to go underground than seek approval from the government, as they viewed the registration requirement to be a violation of their freedom to worship.

IN THEIR
OWN WORDS

"The soldiers told us to quit that religion or else we would be in prison our entire life."

—A YOUNG PENTECOSTAL MAN,
arrested in 2006 for praying with
other believers during mandatory
national service at the Sawa military camp

"They punished me for being a Pentecostal Christian: they beat me, handcuffed my hands and feet together, threw water on me ... they burned my Bible ... Every time they saw me reading it, they would beat me, punish me. There were so many people there, not just me, for two weeks, with a policeman guarding us, lying in the sun."

—A MILITARY POLICEMAN
at the Sawa military camp,
who was punished for his religious beliefs

"As Christians, we must stand with our brothers and sisters in Eritrea. We must show our love not only in prayer, but by standing with them. We must tell the world."

—DANIEL,
Eritrean Christian activist and refugee

"I truly believe that fear and the gospel do not go together, and I was determined that no matter what happened, I would still continue to do God's work."

—HELEN BERHANE,
Eritrean gospel singer

CRACKDOWN

For a short time after the government decreed that only four religious groups were permitted in Eritrea, unregistered Christians gathered in their own homes, joining with other church members for their usual services. But then, in 2003, the government cracked down on these "illegal" groups. They broke into house churches, arrested Christians, and destroyed the religious materials on site.

For example, in just the first few months of the year, one hundred seventy men, women, and children were arrested when police raided several worship services and a wedding ceremony. The believers, accused of practicing "a new religion," were held without charge in cramped, suffocating cells—some of them for up to two weeks—before police released them.

In September, police stormed a house church gathering in Eritrea's capital, Asmara, and arrested twelve young believers—all of them Christians from the Dubre Bethel Church. The Christians—six men and six women—were held at the police station where they were pressured to sign a document denying their faith. They refused, even though the police chief ordered that their food rations be withheld.

By the end of 2003, hundreds of evangelical believers were imprisoned for their religious beliefs in nine known locations across the country. Why did the government perceive evangelical Christians worshiping outside the four approved religious groups to be such a threat? Were these not peace-loving citizens, who cared for their country and wanted to serve their fellow man? Some human rights groups believe authorities may have started the crackdown when they witnessed members of unregistered minority religions attempting to avoid the country's mandatory national or military service.

Whatever the reasons, the PFDJ did not relent in their campaign against unregistered Christians. Even Christian materials were viewed as items to be eliminated. In March 2005, a Christian literature publishing company was closed down. It was later reopened, but only after the government demanded they receive permission before publishing Christian material. Early the next year, a music shop selling Christian albums was closed down and the staff was detained.

Even the registered church is not free from repression from the PFDJ. In January 2006, the leader of the Eritrean Orthodox Church, Abune Antonios, was placed under house arrest after he criticized the government's activity within the church and openly protested the imprisonment of three priests. The church leader, who is in his eighties, continues under house arrest today. There remains concern for his health as he suffers from diabetes and is likely still without access to proper medication.

Unwavering Conviction

Today, arrests and closures continue in Eritrea—and the government does not appear to be softening their hard-line stance and policies. President Isaias Afewerki and his government deny the claims of human rights abuses and insist that Eritrea is a secular country that respects freedom of religion. But the mistreatment of Christians proves otherwise—and the continuing arrests speak to a regime fearful of citizens who obey God rather than man.

Persecution from the state is indeed an ongoing reality in Eritrea and recent events suggest that this may continue to be the case for the near future. In October 2009, ten believers were arrested after security forces raided the home of Pastor Tewelde Hailom, the founding elder of the Full Gospel Church in Asmara. Two of the men arrested were later taken to a police station notorious for its poor conditions for prisoners.

In 2010, seventeen young soldiers carrying out their compulsory national military service were arrested for gathering together for prayer. In

April, another twenty-five believers from the Full Gospel Church were seized.

Only a few months later, in October, the governor of the southern province, Mustafa Nur Hussein, ordered an end-of-year "purge" against Christians. In one of the subsequent raids, authorities uncovered a list of underground church members in three towns and several smaller villages in the area. Security forces used the list to pursue all known believers and their families. On December 31, the entire congregation of the Philadelphia Church in Asmara were arrested. The forty-one members were brought to a police station where they were beaten by authorities.

The crackdown continued in the early weeks of 2011. On January 1, New Year's Day, twenty-seven believers belonging to various underground churches near Asmara were detained by officials. Another thirty-five believers worshiping at a privately owned property in the eastern town of Nakfa were arrested on January 9. Two of the arrested Christians were elderly men in poor health. At the time of this writing, the whereabouts and condition of these imprisoned Christians was not known.

The beginning of 2011 also brought another blow to the Christian community: two more Christians passed away after suffering mistreatment in the country's infamous detention centers.

On January 1, a twenty-seven-year-old woman, Seble Hagos Mebrahtu, died at the Sawa military camp after being refused treatment for malaria. She was reportedly tortured by authorities for the "crime" of reading a Bible in her home. A forty-two-year-old Christian man also passed away after being denied medical treatment.

As of this writing—as unrest and protests sweep across African countries like Tunisia, Yemen, and Egypt—religious liberty experts are keeping a close watch on Eritrea. In his rule, President Afewerki has not allowed the citizens of Eritrea to mobilize themselves for any purpose other than those which are state-sanctioned. How far is he willing to go to ensure Eritrea doesn't follow

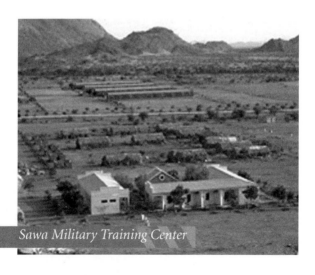

Sawa Military Training Center

the same revolution as other African countries? It is possible he may lash out against unregistered religious groups or any other perceived dissidents in order to maintain control.

Eritrean believers are fully aware of the risks in serving their Savior, yet many of them continue to stand strong in their convictions and their struggle for freedom. Their devotion to the Lord is unwavering, even in the midst of severe oppression and tyranny.

A PRISONER'S SONG

While in prison, her future known only by God, Helen Berhane penned the words to the following song:

Our father Abraham traveled three days to sacrifice his son
From Philistia to the land of Moriah.
That place witnessed Abraham's reward.
He had no regrets on his first day,
No regrets on the second day,
And no regrets on the third day.
His determination was amazing,
The trip to Moriah was extraordinary.
God still has faithful followers,
Promise-keepers who stand firm on his Word.
The God of Abraham is faithful,
He is faithful enough to keep his word.

> *Christianity costs you your life*
> *But at the end, its outcome is victory.*

Faithful servants who refused to be persuaded by the king's reward
Resolved not to defile themselves with the king's food.

They looked better nourished than all the other
young men
And were able to stand before the kings.

Christianity costs you your life
But at the end, its outcome is victory.

The beatings of the Hebrews with the whip was
awful.
The waves of the sea and the mighty wind
Crushed by the stone, suffering by day and by
night;
Paul's faithfulness was tested by a sword.

Christianity costs you your life
But at the end, its outcome is victory.

The journey of Ruth was a hope where there was
no hope;
A sacrifice was paid even for a despised tribe.
Although there was nothing promised for Ruth
By faith she made her way towards Nazareth
And she entered into Jesus' genealogy.

Christianity costs you your life
But at the end, its outcome is victory.

ALEM'S
STORY

Alem lives in a refugee camp in northern Ethiopia, but his family is still in Eritrea. To make a living, he runs a small cafe in the camp selling tea and snacks. He learned the restaurant business back in his native Eritrea. In fact, it was through the witness of the restaurant owner where he worked that he came to faith in Christ in 1987.

In 1996, after eighteen months' military service, Alem made his way to the capital, Asmara, where he enjoyed fellowship as part of a church cell group. Then in 1998, following a recall to the military, he was stationed in Assab, a port on the eastern seaboard of Eritrea. Here, as in other parts of the country, Christians were already coming under pressure for their faith.

When he could, Alem joined with several Christian friends to pray and fast for revival among his colleagues in the military, a practice he continued when he moved back to Asmara in 2001 and became a member of the Kale Hiwot (Word of Life) Church.

Alem is a patriotic and experienced soldier whose ability and skills were valued by his military colleagues. But in 2005 they presented him with a stark ultimatum: "Give up your faith or go to prison."

Alem had already made the choice and replied that he would continue to follow Christ. He was promptly arrested and sent to prison.

For much of his imprisonment, Alem was incarcerated at Mai Serwa. Held in a shipping container, Alem suffered from lack of air, extreme heat, lice, and pain. "Most of the time they would keep us locked up inside the containers," Alem said. "The shipping containers are not very big, only twenty feet long, and many of them with around fifteen to twenty people inside. They normally allowed us out twice a day to go to the toilet. The rest of the time we weren't allowed out. It was very difficult, especially if you were sick or had diarrhea."

Christian prisoners are constantly subjected to mindless and almost futile hard labor for hours at a time in the heat of the day. The guards often humiliate the prisoners, constantly deny them basic human rights, seek to demoralize them, and regularly devise new ways to rob the prisoners of any vestige of dignity in an effort to break their spirit and have them renounce their faith.

But through God's grace, Alem was able to overcome the horrors of the camp. "We liked to praise our God by singing," he explained. "If the guards heard us they got angry, opened the doors of the container and dragged out those they thought were responsible and beat them using batons. Sometimes we could see other Christians being beaten through the small air vent in the side of the container, and we would pray and cry out to God."

Alem also tried to spread the Good News to others. He read Scripture to fellow prisoners from a Bible he smuggled into their shipping container.

Alem is now living in relative safety in a refugee camp, but life still remains difficult. "I have two burdens," he explained. "The first is that I might remain faithful to God and the second concerns my wife and my two children. My wife has said that she cannot accept my faith. She said that if I will sign the form stating I will no longer be a Christian, then we will be able to be together. Otherwise we cannot, and we should be divorced. I want them to believe in God and for us to be reunited as a family."

Pray for Alem and the other Eritrean believers who have fled to refugee camps. Pray for enduring faith amid difficulty. Pray that Alem's wife and children will turn to the Lord and that one day they will be reunited.

ESCAPING ERITREA

Every week, up to five hundred Eritreans risk the dangers of minefields, crocodile-inhabited rivers, and border guards who've been instructed to "shoot to kill," just in the hopes of finding refuge in a neighboring country. Tens of thousands of other Eritreans have already taken this perilous journey. Some have found freedom, some of been forcibly returned, and others have never even made it past their country's borders.

Most who dare to flee Eritrea have to do so alone: husbands have had to leave behind wives and children; sons and daughters may not even have said goodbye to their parents. President Afewerki's paranoid authoritarian rule has ripped thousands of families apart.

Refugees

Those who successfully escape are often unwilling to be publicly identified for fear that the Eritrean authorities will detain their loved ones. If the authorities find out that an Eritrean has fled, the individual's whole family will be targeted. They may be heavily fined and risk losing their land if they don't pay. Sometimes family members are even thrown into prison.

Many Eritreans who do escape find a temporary home in one of the refugee camps in Sudan or Ethiopia. It is estimated that some 160,000 Eritreans now live in Sudan. Tens of thousands of others have fled across the border into northern Ethiopia. From there, many attempt to move on to nearby countries like Libya or Egypt or make their way to Europe. Some who are granted asylum eventually travel to North America. Some Eritreans even risk crossing the Sahara Desert in order to reach Libya.

For those who reach the camps, life remains far from secure. In Sudan, for example, refugees expecting a better life often instead find camps which lack food, security, and healthcare. Refugee children rarely receive a proper education to prepare for their future. Many Eritreans end up venturing away from the camps and into the cities, seeking any work so they can provide for themselves and their families.

Sadly, some Eritreans who have made it to refugee camps have been forcibly returned to Eritrea. Sudan is reported to have occasionally turned a blind eye to the abduction and repatriation of Eritreans by Eritrean officials and spies. Sudanese officials have been known to exploit Eritrean refugees for money. Some refugees who don't have money have been forcibly returned to Eritrea.

In Egypt, refugees are known to have faced opposition from authorities and illegal traffickers. In June 2008, Egypt repatriated 1,200 Eritreans who had traveled into the country from Sudan. In early 2009 another forty-five were sent back to Eritrea within a two-week period. As recently as December 2010, traffickers in Egypt kidnapped 250 Eritrean refugees and demanded an $8,000 ransom for each person.

For many, the benefits of escaping Eritrea's harsh regime outweigh the risks. Yet life for many remains difficult. For Christian refugees, life within the camps has not stopped their witness; they try to bring light into the darkness of their situation by trusting in God and telling others in the camp about Him.

ABEBA'S STORY

Abeba and her four children are among the hundreds of people who have fled from Eritrea each week into neighboring Sudan and Ethiopia. She fled after the death of her husband, Endryas.

Abeba and Endryas were members of the evangelical Kale Hiwot Church. But when the government closed down their church, they began using their home for secret prayer meetings.

Before long, one of their neighbors who was in the security service told authorities about the meetings. The authorities came and took Endryas away to a prison where guards tried to force him to renounce his faith in Christ. He refused. As punishment, the guards severely beat him.

Nearly six months later, Abeba received a phone call that forever changed her life. An official told her she must come to the hospital quickly because Endryas was sick. When she arrived, her husband was already dead.

Abeba learned from the doctors that Endryas, who suffered from diabetes, had died because he had run out of his insulin medicine. Soon afterwards, Abeba and her four children fled from Eritrea. Because of the repression of Christians in Eritrea, they have had to leave their home.

CONCLUSION:
USE YOUR FREEDOM

Today, as you read this, an estimated 2,000 to 3,000 believers are imprisoned in Eritrea for their faith in Jesus Christ. Hundreds of other "dissenters" in the country are also being held, many without charge, for an undisclosed duration.

What does President Afewerki, who calls himself a "Christian" and is a member of the Eritrean Orthodox Tewahedo Church, have to fear from Christians in his country? Are they not peaceful, hardworking, honest? Some sources believe it is not religion in and of itself that Afewerki fears, but rather the thought that religion could rally the people to a cause other than his own.

This fear is particularly heightened by the youth of the country, who are increasingly becoming members of evangelical and Pentecostal denominations. In Eritrea, where national or military service is mandatory, the thought of young people gathering together for purposes other than bolstering the state makes the Eritrean authorities incredibly nervous.

Another possible fear is that if Christian groups evangelize openly, it could disrupt the nearly equal balance between the Muslim and Christian populations in the country. Afewerki is perhaps concerned that communal violence might break out among the over five million people in Eritrea should either Christianity or Islam become more prominent. But Afewerki's fears have grown into paranoia—his people are imprisoned in their own country in order to bring him a sense of security.

Regardless of the reasons behind the widespread persecution, the reality is that Christians in Eritrea today have been denied the freedom to worship the Lord and tell others about Him. Other freedoms, like freedom of speech and freedom of assembly, have also been quashed by the regime of President Afewerki. Since gaining its independence, Eritrea has become one of the most restricted countries in the world today.

Use Every Opportunity

In her book, *Song of the Nightingale* (available

Helen Berhane

through The Voice of the Martyrs), Helen Berhane writes, "I want to give a message to those of you who are Christians and live in the free world: you must not take your freedom for granted. Use every opportunity to praise the Lord every day. If I could sing in prison, imagine what you can do for God's glory with your freedom."

VOM offices around the world are taking action in raising awareness and support for our suffering Eritrean brothers and sisters. Eritrean refugees in Ethiopia are assisted so that they can start their own small business and build a new life for themselves and their families. Bibles and other Christian materials are distributed to refugees so that they might grow in faith and share the Good News with others. Petitions have been distributed in several countries to bring the plight of Eritreans to the attention of government officials in free countries.

So what can you do with your freedom to praise God by helping believers who are suffering in Eritrea today? You can use your freedom to pray with others, bringing to the Lord the pleas of suffering Christians in Eritrea. Pray that imprisoned Christians in Eritrea will be strong in their faith. Pray that God will provide for their friends and family members left behind. Pray that God will break through the fear of President Afewerki and the other leaders in Eritrea, bringing them to repentance and fellowship with Him. Pray that, one day, freedom of religion will be respected for all Eritreans.

You can use your freedom to learn about and share with others the reality of persecution in the world today. Tell your friends and family about Eritrea. Many have not even heard of the country, let alone the situation for Christians there. Write letters to your government representatives. Write letters of encouragement to prisoners themselves by visiting The Voice of the Marytrs' letter-writing website at www.PrisonerAlert.com. Keep informed by subscribing to The Voice of the Martyrs' monthly newsletter (see contact information on the following pages) and consider getting involved in their campaigns and projects that support Eritreans.

You can use your freedom to raise a voice for those whose freedoms have been taken away. What else can you do today for God's glory?

EPILOGUE:
FREE IN CHRIST

Christians in Eritrea continue to be a people imprisoned. But shipping containers and underground cells cannot hinder the freedom they have in Christ.

At the time of this writing, sources reported the deaths of three more Christians who were imprisoned for their faith. The death of these three brings the total number of Christians who have perished in prison to over twenty.

Angesom Teklom Habtemichel, a twenty-six-year-old Christian, died in August 2011 after serving two years in a military camp. He contracted severe malaria but was denied medical treatment because of his written refusal to recant his Christian faith. He passed away one week later.

Just months later, two women died in the Adersete Military Camp in western Eritrea, as they were confined in a dungeon-like cell intended for religious prisoners. Twenty-eight-year-old Terhase Gebremichel Andu and Ferewine Genzabu Kifly, twenty-one, both employees of a wholesale store, were arrested in 2009 during a prayer meeting at a private home. After two years of physical torture and the denial of medical care, the women succumbed to starvation and poor health. Terhase died on October 16 while Ferewine passed away on October 23.

While we grieve with the friends and families of these sisters and brother in Christ, we rejoice that these believers are now free of their bonds and are experiencing complete freedom with Jesus Christ.

All of us were once a people imprisoned, held captive by the bonds of sin and death. Praise the Lord for the gift of freedom we have in Christ —freedom in spite of the sufferings we must endure for a little while until we meet Him face to face. Until that day, please pray for freedom in Eritrea. Pray that the prison doors will be opened and the chains will be loosed (Acts 16:26). But above all, pray that God's freedom will penetrate the hearts of many in Eritrea, liberating them from darkness into light.

To God be the glory!

FOR FURTHER READING

The following sources, a selection of those consulted in the writing of this book, are recommended for further reading and research.

Amnesty International. "Eritrea: 'You Have No Right To Ask.'" <www.amnesty.org/en/library/info/AFR64/003/2004/en>. Accessed August 2, 2011.

Berhane, Helen. 2009. *Song of the Nightingale.* England: Authentic Media.

De Waal, Alexander. 1991. *Evil Days: Thirty Years of War and Famine in Ethiopia.* New York: Human Rights Watch.

Hastings, Adrian. 1994. *The Church in Africa, 1450–1950.* Oxford: Clarendon Press.

Marcus, Harold G. 1994. *A History of Ethiopia.* Berkeley: University of California Press.

Marshall, Paul A. 2008. *Religious Freedom in the World.* Lanham, MD: Rowman & Littlefield Publishers, Inc.

Pankhurst, Richard. 1997. *The Ethiopian Borderlands.* Lawrenceville, NJ: The Red Sea Press, Inc.

Sundkler, Bengt and Christopher Steed. 2000. *A History of the Church in Africa*. New York: Cambridge University Press.

Other Resources

The Voice of the Martyrs monthly newsletter and websites:

    www.persecution.com (USA)
    www.persecution.net (Canada)

Release Int'l: www.releaseinternational.org

Open Doors International: www.opendoors.org

World Evangelical Alliance Religious Liberty Commission: www.worldevangelicals.org/commissions/rlc

Human Rights Watch: www.hrw.org

U.N. Refugee Agency: www.unhcr.org

RESOURCES

The Voice of the Martyrs has many books, videos, brochures, and other products to help you learn more about the persecuted church. In the U.S., to request a resource catalog, order materials, or receive our free monthly newsletter, call (800) 747-0085 or write to:

The Voice of the Martyrs
P.O. Box 443
Bartlesville, OK 74005-0443
www.persecution.com
thevoice@persecution.com

If you are in Australia, Canada, New Zealand, South Africa, or the United Kingdom, contact:

Australia:
Voice of the Martyrs
P.O. Box 250
Lawson NSW 2783
Australia

Website: www.persecution.com.au
Email: thevoice@persecution.com.au

Canada:
Voice of the Martyrs, Inc.
P.O. Box 608
Streetsville, ON L5M 2C1
Canada

Website: www.persecution.net
Email: thevoice@persecution.net

New Zealand:

Voice of the Martyrs
P.O. Box 5482
Papanui, Christchurch 8542
New Zealand

Website: www.persecution.co.nz
Email: thevoice@persecution.co.nz

South Africa:

Christian Mission International
P.O. Box 7157
1417 Primrose Hill
South Africa

Email: cmi@icon.co.za

United Kingdom:

Release International
P.O. Box 54
Orpington BR5 9RT
United Kingdom

Website: www.releaseinternational.org
Email: info@releaseinternational.org